PUBLIC
LIBRARY
ASSOCIATION
A division of the American Library Association

THE GUIDE TO
BASIC COVER LETTER WRITING

Job and Career Information Services
Committee of the Adult
Lifelong Learning Section

Public Library Association
American Library Association

Steven Provenzano

Printed on recyclable paper

VGM Career Horizons
a division of *NTC Publishing Group*
Lincolnwood, Illinois USA

Library of Congress Cataloging-in-Publication Data

Provenzano, Steven.
      The guide to basic cover letter writing / Steven Provenzano.
           p. cm.
      "Job and Career Information Services Committee of the Adult
Lifelong Learning Section, Public Library Association, American
Library Association."
      Includes bibliographical references.
      ISBN 0-8442-8196-4
      1. Cover letters. 2. Résumés (Employment) I. Public Library
Association. Job and Career Information Services Committee.
II. Title.
HF5383.P735   1995
808'.06665--dc20   94-17234
                                                  CIP

1997 Printing
Published by VGM Career Horizons, a division of NTC Publishing Group
4255 West Touhy Avenue
Lincolnwood (Chicago), Illinois 60646-1975, U.S.A.
© 1995 by The Public Library Association/American Library Association.
All rights reserved. No part of this book may be reproduced,
stored in a retrieval system, or transmitted in any form or by any means,
electronic, mechanical, photocopying, recording, or otherwise,
without the prior permission of NTC Publishing Group.
Manufactured in the United States of America.

7 8 9 0 ML 9 8 7 6 5 4 3

Contents

Foreword

When you are starting a job search, where is the first place you should look?

Is it the newspaper's want ad section? A career counselor? The placement office at your school? An employment agency? All of these sources have advantages, but there's another place you should look first.

The place to begin your job search is your local public library. Public libraries are your one-stop source for information on how to launch a successful job search. You can find books on resume writing or career selection and you may even find videos on how to interview successfully.

The public library can be your partner throughout your career. The library can provide current economic information, ideas for improving your company's products or services, or help in launching your own business. Your public librarian can be one of your greatest assets as you pursue your professional life.

For all these reasons, the Public Library Association is proud to work with VGM Career Horizons on this book.

George Needham
Executive Director
Public Library Association

Preface

Before we begin, I wanted to give you some of my own personal tips on writing cover letters.

Before you write your cover letter, visit your favorite library and do some research on the employer and industry that you are considering. Ask your librarian for assistance in finding articles in local or national newspapers and magazines. Are there any references on CD-ROM available, such as Infotrac or the American Business Directory? Business directories also describe the type of work going on at specific locations and give the names of key officials. Always check the accuracy of all information with a phone call. A great cover letter can miss the target if addressed to the wrong person at an old address!

Of course, look at the best and the newest books on cover letters that are available in your library. Consider visiting a larger library or bookstore if your local library or bookstore lacks a large enough selection.

Look at the examples of words, sentences, and forms of letters. Can any of these examples be included in your cover letter? What changes need to be made to reflect your current situation? Be careful not to use the same phrases that everyone is using in their letters. Try to customize and improve all examples that come from books or other sources of information.

Imagine that you are looking at the person to whom you are writing: what words would you use to open the conversation? What details about your past experiences would be most important to focus on to create the proper first impression that will never be forgotten?

Always follow up letters with phone calls within two weeks of mailing to make sure there are no communication problems. *Consider delivering your letter in person, when appropriate.* Ask your librarian about community services for help with resumes or cover letters. Find the closest public library that has a career center or career specialist on staff. You may also contact the Public Library Association or any of the Job and Career Information Services Committee members listed in this book.

Good luck in your job hunt! I hope that you find a personally fulfilling position quickly.

Steve Oserman
Co-chair
Job and Career Information Services Committee
Public Library Association
American Library Association

Acknowledgments

The Job and Career Information Services Committee, Adult Lifelong Learning Section, Public Library Association, a division of the American Library Association, assisted in the preparation of *The Guide to Basic Cover Letter Writing*. Members of the committee who contributed materials are:

Steve Oserman (co-chair)	Skokie (Illinois) Public Library
Ruth Schwab (co-chair)	Ossining (New York) Public Library
Marianne Fairfield	Cuyahoga County (Ohio) Public Library
Vera Green	Carnegie Library of Pittsburgh (Pennsylvania)
Margaret Herman	El Paso (Texas) Public Library
Joan Jackson	San Francisco (California) Public Library
Martin Jaffe	Cuyahoga County (Ohio) Public Library, Maple Heights Regional Branch
Mark Leggett	Indianapolis–Marion County (Indiana) Public Library
James Lyons	St. Louis (Missouri) Public Library
Theodore Mason	East Chicago (Indiana) Public Library
Erlinda Regner	Harold Washington Library (Chicago, Illinois)
Frances Roehm	Bloomington (Illinois) Public Library
Sue Schlaf	Schaumburg Township (Illinois) District Library

Introduction

This book is designed to work in tandem with *The Guide to Basic Resume Writing,* now used by thousands of libraries. The cover letter is an essential part of the job search, because a resume alone cannot highlight a person's individual style the way a cover letter can.

An effective cover letter and resume can greatly increase your chances of getting a better position sooner, and can even result in higher pay and better working conditions. Of course, the ideas and cover letter examples contained in this book will be helpful only to the extent that you make an effort to use them.

The cover letter allows the job applicant to discuss the needs of the company, rather than just the applicant's own need for a position. It gives the job applicant a forum for personalizing each application, while targeting specific companies through research and a customized approach.

An investment of time and effort to write a high-quality cover letter is an investment in your future. Take the time to read through most, if not all, of the cover letter examples in this book. There may be sentences, wordings, or phrases that apply to your situation, and you can use these in your own cover letter to market your abilities and to tell employers why you want to work specifically for them.

If this book is your own personal copy, you can underline sentences and information that you feel would be most helpful, and return to those sections when writing your own cover letter. It is this extra effort and determination that employers are looking for, and it can help you produce a winning cover letter and expand your employment opportunities for a brighter future.

PART I

General Information About Cover Letters

The Purpose of the Cover Letter

This book will demonstrate methods for writing and using an effective cover letter for use in your job search. Along with the following instructions, be sure to review the numerous examples of cover letters that follow.

While you probably know the importance of having an effective resume that demonstrates your qualifications, you may have heard much less about the importance of a well-written cover letter. Yet the cover letter is an essential part of your job search. It is used primarily to:

- Introduce yourself and the resume that follows.

- Show employers that you understand their company/ organization, and have at least a basic knowledge of their products, services, markets, and/or employment needs.

- Tell employers why and how your qualifications can help their specific business or organization: for example, increase sales, reduce costs, or improve efficiency.

- Expand on key points listed in an advertisement or job description. You can use wording directly from the advertisement for this purpose.

- Request an interview to discuss matters that could be of mutual interest, or tell the reader that you'll call *him or her* to discuss the position and arrange a meeting.

Personalize Your Presentation

A resume alone cannot highlight your personal skills the way a cover letter can. A well-written cover letter allows you to discuss the needs of the *company,* rather than your own needs, and give several key reasons why you should be interviewed for the position. You must clearly demonstrate how you would apply your skills, training, and/ or experience to help an organization achieve its goals better than anyone else.

The letter helps convey those personal qualities and desires that may not belong in your resume, such as self-motivation, desire to travel or relocate, or excellent record of attendance. A good letter sets you apart from applicants who submit only resumes or applications. It gives you a way to personalize each resume you send, while targeting companies through research and a customized approach. Your cover letter must focus the reader on your particular skills and provide good reasons to continue reading the resume and/or application that follows.

Employers Need to Know: What Can You Do for Me?

Always keep in mind the employers want to see what *you* can do for *them*. After all, this is why employers are reading your letter and resume in the first place. Too many people writing cover letters discuss only what they want in a position. Of course, what you want in a job—and why you're sending them information about you—is very important. But you must then tell employers how your skills can help them achieve their goals. In other words, the content of your cover letter needs to be a combination of what you want in a job and how the employers will benefit by hiring you.

Here's a tip that can help save time and make it easy to personalize your cover letters: After reading the instructions in this book and checking the cover letter examples, write a cover letter that emphasizes the primary skills and abilities you would like to use most on the job *and* which you feel are valuable to most of the employers who'll be reading your letter. To customize your letters, first address each of them to the hiring authority (call the company if possible to find this, or simply use the name/designation in the advertisement or job listing). Then rewrite the *first* paragraph of the cover letter and mention the company and aspects of the position about which you're most interested.

You should also consider writing a generic or boiler-plate cover letter. Use this letter for responding to blind-box or P.O. box advertisements which don't allow you to research the company or direct your letter to a person. Keep copies of this letter on hand and simply address them to "Dear Hiring Authority," "Dear Hiring Manager," or "Ladies/Gentlemen." Don't forget to sign your letters before enclosing them with your resume or application.

Part of a Targeted Job Search

The current job market may be the most competitive in recent history. There are simply too many applicants for too few well-paying, skilled, or semi-skilled positions. This is why employers now place such a strong emphasis on cover letters and resumes as their first impression of an applicant's skills, abilities, and overall experience.

This is also why employers appreciate a targeted job search: Employers need to feel that you took the time and effort to target their company specifically, and that you take a special interest in working for them. This method of finding job interviews is usually much more effective than the shotgun approach of sending out impersonal resumes or applications to hundreds of companies. See the bibliography at the end of this book for materials on job hunting, correct use of resumes and cover letters, and interviewing to expand your knowledge of effective job hunting strategies.

Most letters and resumes get only a few seconds of attention from busy personnel staff or hiring managers, and you must get your point across promptly and clearly. Your cover letter must have clarity and impact, but must also be grammatically correct and easy for readers to absorb quickly at a glance. That's why most samples in this book are intentionally short and to the point.

Whatever type of cover letter you produce, make sure you proofread it very carefully. Show it to family, friends, and business associates and get their opinions. Nothing turns off an employer more than a cover letter or resume with mistakes such as bad spelling, poor grammar, or hard-to-read type. We'll cover all these areas later in this book.

PART II

Essential Guidelines for Writing Cover Letters

The Basics of Writing a Cover Letter

Your cover letter can follow any of the general formats shown in this book, but most importantly, it must always include the following elements:

1. Who you are: Your name, address, and telephone number with area code.

2. Why you're sending the employer the cover letter. State clearly your intention in sending the letter, and the actual title of the job you're seeking (or the general type of work you're looking for), such as Warehouse Operations, Shipping/Receiving, Accounting or Bookkeeping, or Sales/Marketing. Use the advertisement or job description whenever possible to help write this portion. If that's unavailable, use a more general approach, such as, "I am seeking a position in which I may better utilize my experience in . . ."

3. A short summary of major accomplishments and achievements at various companies, when appropriate, or an outline of your most important training and education. List key skills, abilities or training that applies to the position at hand, such as "experienced in the setup of warehouse fixtures," or "skilled in inventory control and stocking on computer systems," or "have a strong aptitude for figures and utilize ten-key calculators," or "have successful experience in new business development and account management."

4. A short but detailed review or sample of what you know about the company or industry: its products, customers, markets, and its way of doing business. Mention that you want to work specifically for that company.

5. Whether you are willing to travel or relocate, if this a requirement of the position, as in outside sales or driving. You may omit this if it is not requested, or if you *are not* willing to travel or relocate.

6. Other specifics about yourself or the job. If someone at the company suggested you send your application, mention that person's name. If the posting asks you to include salary requirements, and not salary history, give them a desired salary range and avoid a specific number. For example, you might say "ten to twelve dollars per hour, negotiable." You may include this in a letter, but if both salary requirements and salary history are requested, include them on a separate salary history sheet, and end the page by saying, "Salary requirements are open to negotiation."

7. Thank the reader for his or her time and/or c
let him or her know that you look forward to

Overall Format

There are several formats for cover letters presented in this boo
most consist of an introductory paragraph, the body of the text, and
a closing. All of the examples have plenty of white space; that is,
space between paragraphs and before and after the text. This makes
them easier to read and pleasing to the eye.

Some examples contain "bullet points" which help draw the eye
and the reader's attention. You should consider this format if you
have short, key accomplishments or some highly important or
successful experience. Simply highlight the information by placing
an asterisk, dash, circle, or box before the sentence.

You can easily change these bullet points to target specific jobs
and develop those aspects of your background you feel are most
important to any certain job. In this example, the second paragraph
is followed with bulleted items:

I am exploring opportunities as General Office Assistant with your company. I'm especially
interested in a position that offers the potential for greater challenge and career growth.

My most recent position required extensive customer relations, as well as data entry and retrieval
on an IBM system. Because of this experience, I can now offer your company:

*   Proficiency in WordPerfect 5.1 and Lotus 1-2-3, as well as a strong aptitude for learning other
    computer software.

*   Experience in operating a 10-line Voicecom switchboard while taking messages and scheduling
    appointments.

*   A proven ability to handle customer problems and a wide range of duties in a tactful,
    professional manner.

I would welcome the opportunity to speak with you personally to discuss how my background can
benefit your company. I am willing to relocate for the right opportunity, and can provide excellent
references at your request.

Thank you for your time and consideration. I look forward to hearing from you soon.

Sincerely,

Wilma Jones

enclosure

In this example, notice how the writer's key skills and abilities stand
out from the rest of the letter. You may also notice how the eye is
quickly drawn to the bulleted material.

General Procedure

1. Always send a cover letter with your resume and personalize it by researching the company. Exceptions can be made for blind box ads. Include a letter addressed to "Ladies/Gentlemen," "Dear Hiring Authority," or "Dear Prospective Employer."

2. Address your letters to an individual whenever possible. If you don't have a name, call the company and get the exact spelling of the hiring authority's name and the person's job title. If that's not available, send it to the personnel manager, human resources representative or corporate recruiter, with his or her name if possible.

3. If you make your letters brief and to the point, they will stand a much better chance of getting read. Some employers skip over very long letters, so keep your letter down to three to five short paragraphs to increase its readability.

4. Letters should always be typed. Try to use the same paper color for both resumes and letters, but don't worry too much if they don't match. White goes well with everything, is easy to correct on your typewriter and doesn't look mass produced. It also looks more personal and immediate. If you honestly have no way to get a letter typed, find someone with great handwriting.

5. Proofread your letter as closely as your resume. Proofread once for content, then once for grammar and typing mistakes. Then read it backwards, and have someone else read it, too.

Before You Begin Writing: Research, Research, Research

As mentioned earlier, employers want to know that you've taken the time to review their hiring needs before sending an application, resume, or cover letter. This is all part of your targeted job search. Keep in mind that if you don't have the time or means to conduct a targeted search, you should still write a letter that emphasizes those skills and abilities that could be utilized by *most* companies to which you apply.

To begin your research, first review the job description or advertisement, if any. You may also find a company's annual or quarterly report in the library, or call the company and ask the receptionist about the company's products, services, overall size, and/or markets. Most companies are happy to tell you all about their product lines and ranking in the industry. You can also request or review any brochures or other information on the company. There are several books in the library on publicly held companies, including service or manufacturer directories, produced on a statewide basis. Again, check the bibliography at the end of this book for more information.

Whenever possible, try to get:

1. The hiring authority's precise name and job title.

2. The correct spelling of the company name.

3. The correct address, including suite number, if any, and ZIP code.

Reinforce Key Points of Your Resume

Your resume is a great place to look for words to include in your cover letter. Pull out the most relevant points of your experience and reword them using "I" and "We" for a more personal touch. (If you don't yet have a resume, see the companion volume to this book, *The Guide to Basic Resume Writing*.) Also, check the bibliography at the back of this book for a listing of resume books filled with examples and resume-writing techniques.

If you don't have a resume, take a moment to jot down your most important skills, training, and abilities, whether or not you've done them on the job. Refer to this list when writing your cover letter and insert those items most important to specific positions, perhaps as bulleted points.

Highlight Applicable Skills and Achievements

Once you have an idea about the requirements of the position and the needs of the company, make a list of those qualifications and achievements you believe would be most applicable and valuable to the potential employer. Get a blank piece of paper and start listing items that most apply to the needs of the company(s):

1. Skills learned on the job. Even if you haven't worked at a certain task for several years, list your most applicable skills if you still believe you're qualified and can use them in a new position.

2. Subjects learned in school, but only if you think they are current or important to the position you're seeking.

3. Key accomplishments at previous positions; notable contributions to your previous employers. Perhaps you increased sales (by what percentage?), reduced waste, lowered the cost of production, or raised customer satisfaction.

4. Several of your key personal attributes: Are you self-motivated, energetic, a strong communicator, consistently on-time to work, well-organized, and reliable?

Not all of these points belong in every cover letter. Use those items most relevant to the position. These will change with every letter you write and for every company you approach. When writing a generic cover letter, you can use most or all of these points to help sell your overall qualifications.

General Grammar Rules for Cover Letters

As mentioned earlier, your cover letter must be completely free of errors in grammar and spelling. That's because it is the reader's first impression of who you are, what you can do, and your level of professionalism. Always use clear, concise language, and avoid repeating words. Avoid beginning more than one sentence with the same word, and try to use business terms that might actually be used by the company. Remember that you're trying to portray yourself as being a match for the new position, rather than simply showing that you were well qualified for your previous jobs.

When listing a state as part of your return address, use the appropriate postal code rather than the entire state name; for example, use IL for Illinois.

Keep your sentences short and to the point. It's hard to digest run-on or rambling sentences with little or no punctuation. Use a sentence for each key thought, then simply begin another sentence with related thoughts. The letter must be light and easy to read, yet still have impact and present important information to the reader.

Again, make sure to proofread all your writing carefully before mailing. Have others read it, too. If you find yourself rushing to get something in the mail, take a moment to slow down and make sure you are sending out high-quality information. Your career is in your hands!

Primary Points of Cover Letter Content

Overall, your cover letter should contain only positive aspects of your background and no negatives. Exceptions can be made if you have a specific aspect about your past that must be explained to employers before requesting an interview. For example, you might include reasons for having held several short-term jobs within a one- or two-year period, but only if this happened because of relocation, major company downsizings, layoffs, or your company going out of business, and only if you're otherwise having trouble getting interviews. If you have served time in prison, be sure to see the cover letter example on page 63. Always be sure to highlight the skills you can currently provide; mention but don't dwell on your past.

Never speak badly of your previous employers, either in your letter or during an interview. Instead, try to state that you left your former position because you were looking for new job challenges, better pay, better hours or working conditions, or greater career advancement.

Also avoid listing your salary history or references in your cover letter. These items belong on separate salary history or reference sheets. (For an explanation of this item, see *The Guide to Basic Resume Writing* or similar books.) You may state your most recent wages or salary requirements in your cover letter only if it is requested in an advertisement or by the employer. If you must list salary information, use only ranges: "mid to upper $30s per year" or "lower $20s per year."

Most importantly, your materials must read well, with authority and impact. Don't oversell or undersell your qualifications. Use direct, no-nonsense, easy to understand language.

Remember that cover letters and resumes are designed to get your foot in the door for an interview with an employer so you can present your total qualifications. The interview process is where the details of salary should be discussed.

Formatting Your Letter

The first five of the following cover letter examples are set in a basic typewriter font that prints at ten characters per inch (10 cpi) and use none of the features of modern laser typesetting, such as boldfacing or italics. These letters were included to demonstrate a good format for typewritten letters; however, word-processed or typeset letters are always preferred. The remaining examples are set in 9-point or 10-point proportional typefaces. Proportional typefaces allow you to pack more letters into a smaller space on the page, and they're generally easier to read.

The sample letters below are designed to give you a basis for your own customized letters. The names and addresses of those sending these letters have been changed for confidentiality. You should also write a very general boilerplate letter to send to blind box or P.O. box ads, which list only a box number and no company name. A letter sent to a blind box or P.O. box can be specific about your skills, but does not need to be specific about the company.

Simple block-style letters have no indents or tabs. You can center your name and address on the page to give the appearance of personalized stationery. In the first typewritten example, an extra space between each letter of the person's name gives the illusion of larger type, and helps the name to stand out in the reader's mind.

All other letters in this book are typeset in 9-point American Typewriter Medium, often using **boldface** or *italic*. (In the printing industry, a *point* refers to type size; there are 72 points per inch.) Boldface and italic can help add style and emphasis to your writing, but should not be overused. If you only have access to a typewriter, remember that you can use underlining and CAPITALIZATION to emphasize your name or other key points. You can also place a rule (line) across the top of the page—underneath your name, perhaps—to give your letters visual weight and give the reader a point to focus on.

Remember to read these examples carefully and take notes on a separate sheet of paper. Keep track of sentences and words you can use in your own personalized cover letters.

Professional Printing and Appearance

Once the writing is finished, you should have your resumes printed and your cover letters, if created on a computer, laser-printed. This gives you a professional image and presents you as serious about the job. Most quick printers, professional resume services, and secretarial services will be happy to help you with this, and many can be found in your local yellow pages. Your library may have computers and laser printers available for this task. If you can keep your cover letter and resume on a diskette, updates and changes are fast and easy. Always keep backup copies of both documents on paper, just in case the disk is lost or damaged.

Be sure to print numerous copies of a general letter addressed simply to the Hiring Authority or similar title. Keep these on hand for answering ads with blind box or P.O. box numbers.

Even general letters to blind boxes or P.O. boxes can be personalized by modifying the first two or three paragraphs. Using a typewriter or printer, insert at least the company name and address, and, preferably, any other information that shows you know about the company and how you can help it.

PART III

Cover Letter Examples for Various Positions

The following cover letter examples are separated into groups. The first group contains letters primarily for unskilled and semi-skilled positions, for general employment, or for recent college graduates with little or no work experience. Some of these letters are labeled "boilerplate"; you can modify these to suit your needs. The second group contains letters for skilled tradespersons.

The third group contains letters for professional, management, or other upper-level positions. The fourth group contains letters for people in special situations, such as a woman, retiree, or veteran returning to the work force, a Spanish-speaking applicant seeking basic employment, or a former prison inmate. The section ends with follow-up letters (very important!) and examples of reference and salary history sheets.

Entry-Level, Semi-Skilled, or General Employment

Use words and phrases from the following examples to write your own, customized cover letter. Remember to research the company whenever possible before calling the hiring authority or writing your letter. When you're prepared to discuss the job opportunity, call the company and try to speak directly to the key decision maker. Tell him or her exactly why you're interested in the firm and, if possible, schedule an interview at that time.

If you can't book an interview right away, at least make sure to mention your name clearly to the hiring authority.

Avoid using complex sentences or too many fancy words. Your cover letter will be most effective when you use simple words to communicate important, relevant information. Write at a level your reader can understand and appreciate, and you'll have a much better chance of getting called for an interview.

N A N C Y J. H A R R I S
434 N. Wabash Street
Cleveland, OH 40621
331/555-6845

Dear Hiring Manager:

I am exploring employment opportunities with your company. Specifically, I am seeking to better utilize my experience and training in [your field of experience/interest].

Throughout my career, I've proven my ability to work effectively with management and staff at all levels of experience. Most importantly, I can determine and meet the needs of the customer in a professional, yet personalized, manner.

I can provide excellent references upon request, and am willing to travel for the right opportunity. Please let me know as soon as possible when we may meet for an interview and discuss mutual interests. I look forward to your response.

Thank you for your time and consideration.

Sincerely,

Nancy J. Harris

enclosure

THOMAS F. DEACON
319 Verde Drive
Boulder Heights, CO 30004
208/555-5134

Dear Hiring Executive [or Manager]:

I am exploring the possibility of joining your staff and have enclosed my resume for your review. Specifically, I am seeking to better use my talents in [building maintenance, mechanics, professional driving, production operations, etc].

My background includes training [or experience] in [boiler/HVAC repair; engine rebuilding and tune-ups; on-time deliveries; operation of folders, packers, and cutters; soldering and product assembly; etc]. I've developed excellent relations with [teachers, managers, co-workers, customers], and I feel that this can be valuable to your firm.

I am available for an interview at your convenience to discuss how my education and experience could benefit your company. Please contact me at the above number or address in order to arrange a meeting. I am looking forward to exploring career opportunities with your company.

Thank you for your time and consideration.

Sincerely,

Thomas F. Deacon

enclosure

Sample Letter
General/Entry-Level
Boilerplate

LUCY DISH
9876 College Avenue #213
DeKalb, IL 60115
815/555-2474

Dear Prospective Employer:

In the interest of exploring employment opportunities with your organization, I have enclosed my resume for your review. Specifically, I am seeking to expand my experience (and training) in [office management, accounting, data processing, etc.].

My strong work ethic and attention to detail would prove extremely valuable to a company that makes customer service its top priority. I am self-motivated and energetic, and communicate well with customers, staff, and management to get the job done.

Please let me know as soon as possible when we may meet to discuss mutual interests. Thank you for your time, and I look forward to your response.

Sincerely,

Lucy Dish

enclosure

Sample Letter
General/Entry-Level
New College Graduate

CAESAR G. NASH
21 Wicka Road
Hartland, WI 53029
414/555-5892

May 5, 199_

Dear Hiring Manager:

I am exploring employment opportunities with your company. Specifically, I am seeking to better utilize my ability to train, motivate, and energize both groups and individuals in successful endeavors.

During various volunteer positions in college, I was highly successful in training and coordinating individuals with a wide range of backgrounds. My hands-on work experience includes customer service, sales, and business administration, all with a positive attitude.

I have proven my ability to work effectively with management and staff at all levels of experience. Most importantly, I have demonstrated my ability to determine and meet the needs of the customer in a professional yet personalized manner.

My references are available upon request, and I'm willing to travel for the right opportunity. Please let me know as soon as possible when we may meet for an interview and discuss mutual interests. I look forward to your response.

Thank you for your time and consideration.

Sincerely,

Caesar G. Nash

enclosure

WILLIAM G. STEVENS
21 Nagtown Road
Hartland, WI 53029
414/555-5892

Dear Hiring Manager:

During various volunteer positions in college, I was highly successful in training and coordinating individuals with a wide range of backgrounds. My hands-on work experience includes customer service, sales, and business administration, all with a highly positive attitude.

It was in my Advanced Business class that I first learned of your company, and I would now like to use my ability to train, motivate, and energize groups and individuals in successful endeavors for your company.

Through summer employment, I've proven my ability to work effectively with management and staff at all levels of experience. Most importantly, I have demonstrated my ability to determine and meet the needs of the customer in a professional, yet personalized, manner.

If required, I can provide excellent references, and am willing to travel for the right opportunity. Please let me know as soon as possible when we may meet for an interview and discuss mutual interests. I look forward to your response.

Thank you for your time and consideration.

Sincerely,

William G. Stevens

enclosure

Sample Letter
General Entry-Level
Trucking/Transportation

ALBERT S. POST
810 Oak Drive #4B
Lisle, IL 60532
708/555-1445

Dear Hiring Manager:

I am seeking to better utilize my skills in transportation, developed in positions with UPS and Central Transport. As my resume indicates, I have successful experience in many areas of customer service, dock operations, and freight tracking. I'm especially interested in joining a professional, growth-oriented company.

While attending Central Indiana University, I was also on the Dean's List, served as Assistant Coach for the youth hockey team, and was active in the Society for the Advancement of Management. Being involved in these groups helped to round out my education, and greatly improved my interpersonal communication skills.

I can provide letters of reference from professors and faculty, and am willing to travel for the right opportunity. Please let me know as soon as possible when we may meet for an interview and discuss mutual interests. I look forward to your response.

Sincerely,

Albert S. Post

enclosure

Sample Letter
**General Entry-Level
Mechanic/Litle Training**

GEORGE WEST
1205 Orange Road
Nassau, NY 11736
516/555-0020

Dear Hiring Authority:

I am seeking a position as Mechanic where I may fully utilize my strong aptitude for working with auto and truck engines, transmissions, and related systems.

My interest in auto mechanics began with intensive training in my high-school automotive class, where I learned the basics of repair, troubleshooting, and preventive maintenance.

I've since repaired and completely rebuilt a 1973 Chevrolet Camaro, including full teardown and assembly of a 307-cubic-inch small-block engine. I am very skilled in all types of general automotive maintenance, including:

*   Engine tune-ups, including timing adjustments, belt tightening, spark plug replacement, and replacement of fuel filters and injectors.

*   Inspection and filling of all essential fluids, including oil, brake, power steering, and transmission.

*   Diagnostic checking and replacement of brake shoes and pads, as well as mufflers, shocks, and struts.

In addition to my technical skills, I can bring you a strong work ethic and excellent record of attendance at my high school. Please feel free to call me with any questions you may have, or to arrange a personal interview. I would enjoy meeting with you and your service team.

Thank you for your prompt consideration.

Sincerely,

George West

enclosure

Skilled Tradesperson

With even a small amount of research, you can show the reader why you wish to work for his or her specific company. Remember to address your letter to an individual whenever possible and tell the reader the type of work you're looking for.

In the second paragraph, show points you've learned about the company, its products, facilities, type of operation, etc. Check your resume, job applications, and skill list to emphasize key talents you can bring to the position, especially technical or communication skills sought by the company. Here you can mention such things as proficiency in the use of certain factory equipment, or experience at major construction projects.

Finally, request an interview or tell the hiring authority when you'll call, and remember to thank the reader for his or her time and consideration.

Sample Letter
Skilled Tradesperson
Equipment Repair

STEVEN FIERO
77 Hill Drive
Bloomingdale, IL 60108
708/555-6370

Mr. Robert Jones
General Candy Company
5343 Sugar Lane
Sweetbox, IL 60132

Dear Mr. Jones:

I am exploring opportunities with General Candy Company. Specifically, I would like to better utilize my skills in the repair and operation of a wide range of production equipment, developed with M&M Mars.

My research has shown that you will soon be expanding your chocolate bar production capacity by nearly 20 percent, and I would like to play a part in your company's success.

As you will see by my resume, my background includes full responsiblity for equipment teardown and troubleshooting. I've proven my ability to work closely with staff and management in plant safety and production streamlining, while keeping an eye on overhead. I have an excellent record of attendance and efficiency, and can provide you with references upon request.

Please let me know as soon as possible when we may meet for an interview. I look forward to your response.

Thank you for your time and consideration.

Sincerely,

Steven Fiero

enclosure

Sample Letter
**Skilled Tradesperson
Photocopier Repair**

Sandra M. Smith
East 10118 11th Avenue
Spokane, WA 99225
509/555-1705

Personnel Department
Savin Corporation
3243 N. Evanston Street
Spokane, WA 99225

Dear Personnel Representative:

Given the excellent reputation of Savin Corporation, I have enclosed my resume for your review.

My background includes full responsibility for the teardown, repair, and troubleshooting of virtually all brands of photocopiers to component level. In addition, I have:

* Recently completed training in laser copier technology.

* Successfully trained several employees in direct customer service, system repair, and documentation.

* Earned numerous commendations from customers and supervisors for prompt, effective repairs and reduced service calls.

Throughout my career, I've proven my ability to quickly learn new photocopier systems, and to always stay abreast of the latest technologies. I believe this is essential for keeping positive relations with all customers, while reducing both down time and overhead costs.

I would welcome the chance to meet with you or your technical staff to discuss career opportunities. Please let me know as soon as possible when I could come to your office for an interview.

Sincerely,

Sandra M. Smith

enclosure

Sample Letter
Skilled Tradesperson
Machinist/Shop Worker

STANLEY CAREY
16 Fulton Drive
Streamwood, NY 60107
318/555-4823

Dear Hiring Manager:

With extensive training in shop operations and more than two years of experience as a Machinist, I am certain I can bring your company the skills and devotion to quality required for success.

I have successful experience in lathe, mill, and grinding work for jigs, fixtures, prototypes and one-of-a-kind products.

My background includes full responsibility for job scheduling and supervision, from blueprint reading to finished product quality and customer satisfaction. I can handle a wide range of production duties while reducing waste and overhead costs.

I would welcome the opportunity to meet with you personally regarding your specific shop needs. I can provide references upon request, and look forward to hearing from you soon.

Sincerely,

Stanley Carey

enclosure

Sample Letter
Skilled Tradesperson
Welder

DARCY N. MELLOT
233 Winding Glen Drive
Carol Stream, IL 60188
708/555-5192

Dear Hiring Manager:

Given the solid reputation of your company, I am exploring opportunities as a Maintenance Welder. As a reliable member of your production team, I can offer your company proficiency in:

* ARC, MIG, TIG, Flux-core, and Gas welding for a wide range of products and maintenance welding applications.

* Full project supervision, including welding, assembly, and quality control.

* A strong aptitude for learning how to operate new equipment, while keeping a sharp eye on quality of the finished product.

Because the following resume is only a brief outline of my skills and abilities, I would welcome the chance the meet with you personally and discuss the needs of your particular operation.

I can provide excellent references upon request and am willing to travel for the right opportunity. Please let me know as soon as possible when we may meet for an interview. I look forward to your response.

Thank you for your time and consideration.

Sincerely,

Darcy N. Mellot

enclosure

Sample Letter
Skilled Tradesperson
Casino Worker

JOSEPH EDWARDS
43445 Elm Lane
El Paso, TX 30107
508/555-6201

Mr. Ralph Albertson
Hollywood Casinos
49 West Galena Blvd.
Aurora, CA 43211

Dear Mr. Albertson:

According to a recent article in the *San Francisco Chronicle*, your casino will soon be expanding its operations. I would like to meet with you or your staff to discuss career opportunities with your successful organization.

My background includes experience as Crewman with Fleetwide Marine Corporation. With my knowledge of food and beverage service and management, along with my Crewman's experience and Sanitation Certification, I would be a versatile professional aboard your vessel.

As my resume indicates, I have extensive experience in business administration including staff training, supervision, and the coordination of daily operations. In addition, I am qualified in job scheduling, as well as material and supply purchasing.

I can provide excellent references for your review. I am willing to travel or relocate for the right opportunity. Please let me know as soon as possible when we may meet to discuss any Crewman or Service position available. I look forward to your response.

Thank you for your time and consideration.

Sincerely,

Joseph Edwards

enclosure

LINDA B. WINKLER
3371 Georgian Place
Des Moines, IA 30103
408/555-6113

Dear Hiring Manager:

I can bring your travel agency the strict attention to detail and solid communication skills that are essential to success. My background includes hands-on training and experience in direct customer service, reservations, itinerary planning, and problem solving. Most importantly, I can provide:

* Successful experience in heavy customer service, CRT work, and telephone communications.

* An excellent knowledge of airline rates, routes, and ground services.

* The ability to solve customer problems in a prompt, personalized manner.

I am willing to travel or relocate for the right opportunity and could meet to discuss mutual interests.

Thank you for your time and consideration.

Sincerely,

Linda B. Winkler

enclosure

Sample Letter
Skilled Tradesperson
Drafting/Design

HUNTER S. THOMAS
1330 S. Prospect
Ocala, FL 30143
213/555-7543

Dear Hiring Manager:

My strong attention to detail and aptitude for learning have been the key to my success at College of Ocala, where I recently completed my Associate's Degree in Architectural Drafting and Design. I would now like to utilize my training and skills in either a full-time or apprentice position with your excellent company.

I have consistently demonstrated my ability to learn the latest in computer software while fine-tuning my communication/research skills. Because my resume is only a summary of my background, I would welcome the opportunity to meet with you personally to discuss your specific business operation. I can provide excellent references upon request and look forward to a personal interview at your convenience.

Thank you for your time and consideration.

Sincerely yours,

Hunter S. Thomas

encl.

MATTHEW P. NORDQUIST
1200 N. Rohlwing Road #221
Addison, VA 10101
319/555-4653

Dear Hiring Manager:

Having held positions as Kitchen Manager and Sous Chef with restaurants such as Chez Paul, I am certain I can be an asset to your operation. Specifically, I am seeking to better utilize my skills in staff motivation and supervision in a high quality restaurant, where service and professionalism are the keys to success.

My background includes full responsibility for kitchen operations and sanitation. During my position with Chez Paul, I developed a strong repeat business through strict attention to detail and quality. This resulted in highly favorable reviews in such publications as *The Michelin Guide* and the *Chicago Tribune.*

Prior to Chez Paul, as my resume indicates, I was Sous Chef at Prairie Restaurant, which specialized in American and French cuisine. It was here that I fine-tuned my skills in creative presentations and hearty entrees.

Please let me know as soon as possible when we can discuss how my skills may help enhance your reputation.

Thank you for your time and consideration.

Sincerely,

Matthew P. Nordquist

enclosure

Sample Letter
Skilled Tradesperson
Automobile Sales

LAWRENCE W. JONES
33627 Ash Street
Roselle, TN 51112
638/555-1785

Dear Hiring Manager:

With more than seven years in automobile sales, I am seeking to better utilize my experience in automotive Sales Management, developed in various positions with such dealerships as Celozzi Ettleson and Al Piemonte Ford.

*   My background includes full responsibility for department setup and management, as well as effective closed-door sales. I'm a strong believer in supervision by example, and have proven my ability to motivate workers and increase sales of new and used automobiles, warranties, and aftermarket products.

*   I was directly responsible for over $1 million in gross sales for 1993.

*   Throughout my career, I have proven my ability to expand dealership sales through positive, personalized service to a wide range of clientele.

Please let me know as soon as possible when we may meet for an interview and discuss opportunities for increased profitability at your dealership. I look forward to your response.

Thank you for your time and consideration.

Sincerely,

Lawrence W. Jones

encl.

Sample Letter
Skilled Tradesperson
HVAC Service/Installer

PERRY WRENCH
333 Flagstaff Lane
Golden Estates, NV 51224
428/555-2453

Dear Hiring Manager:

Given the expanding housing market in our portion of the state, the demand for quality HVAC installations and repair has never been greater. I recently received Certification in HVAC systems and am certain my education in state-of-the-art equipment can benefit your customers and your company.

My training from Triton College has given me expertise in:

* Assessment of heating and cooling needs for residential and commercial structures up to 100,000 cubic feet in size.

* The teardown and troubleshooting of air conditioners, gas and electric furnaces, and a wide range of equipment, including humidifiers.

* Dealing with vendors and parts suppliers to tackle custom work with speed and consistently high quality, at the lowest possible cost.

Throughout my employment as a handyman at a small apartment complex, I've proven my ability to work well with customers and provide quick, professional service. I am very self-motivated, with an excellent record of attendance and customer satisfaction.

Please let me know as soon as possible when we may meet for an interview and discuss in detail how my skills may benefit you. I look forward to your response. Thank you for your time and consideration.

Sincerely,

Perry Wrench

enclosure

Sample Letter
Skilled Tradesperson
General Office/Administration

Donald L. Paige
35 Castle Lane
Overland Park, MO 30103
328/555-6718

The Doctors Office
12 Overland Road
Branson, MO 30103

Dear Hiring Physician:

Today's office environment requires speed, accuracy, and strict attention to detail. These are among the many qualifications I can bring to your practice. Specifically, I would like to better utilize my experience in direct patient relations and office administration.

As my resume indicates, I have extensive experience in patient scheduling, billing, and general bookkeeping. Throughout my employment and education, I've developed a strong background in medical/dental terminologies and clinical procedures, essential elements in effective patient care.

Most importantly, I have proven my ability to determine and meet the needs of the patient in a professional yet personalized manner.

I would like to meet for an interview to discuss mutual interests, and can be reached after 6 p.m. on weekdays at the above phone number. I look forward to your response.

Thank you for your time and consideration.

Sincerely,

Donald L. Paige

encl.

Sample Letter
Skilled Tradesperson
Office/Sales Administration

DENISE L. SMITH
147 Foxgrove Road
Bartlett, MI 50103
238/555-6482

Dear Hiring Manager:

My profit-building skills in sales administration, market expansion, and product development could prove highly valuable to a growing, innovative company such as yours.

My background includes the establishment of highly profitable territories, as well as all aspects of product configuration and account management for the sale of household goods. I believe I can improve your company's profitability through market penetration, sales staff training, and/or overall sales managment. During my most recent position I:

* Achieved a 15 percent growth in sales among soft product lines.

* Developed a strong referral business through personalized service, quick troubleshooting, and excellent product knowledge.

Because my resume is necessarily brief, I would welcome the chance to meet with you personally regarding your specific operation and discuss how my skills can expand your market share. I am willing to travel for the right opportunity, and can provide excellent client references at your request.

Thank you for your time and consideration, and I look forward to meeting with you soon.

Sincerely,

Denise L. Smith

enclosure

Sample Letter
Skilled Tradesperson
Clerk/Office Assistant

EDWARD HOLLINGS
87 Meadow Lane
Hanover Park, NM 40103
308/555-3501

Mr. John Richards
John Richards & Associates
390 E. Irving Park Road
Albuquerque, NM 89111

Dear Mr. Richards:

I am exploring opportunities as Office Assistant, and your advertisement in the *New Mexico News* seems perfectly matched to my qualifications. I can bring your company comprehensive analytical and communication skills, as well as a background in data entry and retrieval using Lotus 1-2-3.

As my resume indicates, I have direct experience in cash applications and account reconciliations, as well as a solid background in customer communications and problem solving. I've proven my ability to quickly learn new procedures, while streamlining operations for prompt, accurate customer response.

I can provide excellent references on request, and am willing to travel for the right opportunity. Please let me know as soon as possible when we may meet for an interview and discuss mutual interests. I look forward to your response.

Thank you for your time and consideration.

Sincerely,

Edward Hollings

encl.

LAWRENCE ROBERTS
478 South Oak Drive
Topeka, KS 40103
908/555-5083

Dear Hiring Manager:

Effective customer service is essential to the success of any organization, and I am exploring new opportunities to utilize my experience to benefit your company.

My background includes responsibility for the training and supervision of customer service staff at Indian Lakes Resort. It was here that I fine-tuned my skills in data entry, sales support, and a wide range of office functions. I now seek to better utilize my talents in a challenging environment offering professional growth and stability.

I've proven my ability to use tact and professionalism in working with staff and management, and, most importantly, with virtually all types of customers.

Please let me know as soon as possible when we may meet to discuss mutual interests, or if you require any further information on my background. I look forward to hearing from you soon.

Sincerely,

Lawrence Roberts

enclosure

Sample Letter
Skilled Tradesperson
Administrative Assistant
Referred by Company Employee

SANDRA A. JOHNSON
62 Sandra Court
Lexington, KY 20139
608/555-2515

Edward Albert
Vice President
Total Power Corporation
900 S. Madison Street
Louisville, KY 40292

Dear Mr. Albert:

I am exploring opportunities as Administrative Assistant and heard about your company through Jason Rogers, who suggested I send you my resume.

I am a skilled typist, proficient in WordPerfect 5.1 and Lotus 1-2-3. As my resume indicates, I have highly successful experience in the medical field and with Sears Roebuck & Co. Throughout my career, I've proven my ability to work effectively with management and staff at all levels of experience. Most importantly, I can ensure high customer satisfaction through personalized yet effective communications.

I am eager to join your successful team of professionals. Please let me know as soon as possible when we may meet for an interview and discuss mutual interests. I look forward to your response.

Thank you for your time and consideration.

Sincerely,

Sandra A. Johnson

enclosure

Sample Letter
Skilled Tradesperson
Aircraft Technician/Mechanic

SUSAN PROVENZANO
13420 Wellington Avenue #415
Elk Grove, GA 20007
385/555-7032

Mr. A.B. Sample
President
XYZ Corporation
800 Enterprise Drive, Suite 209
Atlanta, GA 30328

Dear Mr. Sample:

During my military tenure, I saved the Air Force a $1,000 overhaul cost per brake assembly and improved the repair capability at the various shops to which I was assigned. In addition, I developed and successfully administered a nondestructive inspection program. I thrive on the challenge of improving both productivity and systems. I am goal-oriented and professional, and I would like to put my experience to work for you.

If required, please forward an employment application in the enclosed self-addressed, stamped envelope. My credentials include:

* Airframe Mechanic License.

* More than seven years of military aviation experience including positions as Crew Chief and Aircraft Hydraulic Technician/Mechanic.

* Completion of the Aviation Maintenance Technology program through Emby-Riddle Aeronautical University.

* For Outstanding Service and Excellent Performance, I received two Air Force Achievement Medals and one Air Force Commendation Medal.

I'm confident that with my mechanical and technical skills, I would be a valuable asset, and could offer many years of quality service. I appreciate your time and look forward to discussing my qualifications in a personal interview.

Sincerely,

Susan Provenzano

enclosure

JAMES M. WILSON
61 Wood Drive
Carol Lake, AL 31146
596-555-0167

Mr. Robert Smith
Smith and Jones, Inc.
100 E. Front St.
Carol Lake, AL 31146

Dear Mr. Smith:

I am exploring new opportunities in Distribution and/or Shipping operations with your company. Specifically, I would like to utilize my experience with IBM in a challenging new position.

My employment with IBM has greatly expanded my skills in routing, trafficking, and distribution, and I've gained an excellent knowledge of freight carriers, rates, and delivery schedules. Throughout my career, I've proven my abiility to work effectively with management and staff at all levels of experience. Most importantly, I have demonstrated my ability to determine and meet the needs of the customer in fast-paced business environments.

I will be calling you early next week to arrange an interview. Please let me know if there's any further information you require regarding my skills, and how they can be tailored to meet your specific needs. I look forward to meeting you soon.

Thank you for your time and consideration.

Sincerely,

James M. Wilson

enclosure

Sample Letter
Skilled Tradesperson
Security Guard

WILLIAM E. WINKLER
332 W. Amelia
Addison, MT 40101
708/555-0170

Dear Hiring Manager:

A consistent rise in theft at retail operations nationwide prompts me to enclose my resume for your review. I am exploring opportunities in Retail Security, and would like to better utilize my experience in safety, shortage, and security operations, developed with Venture Stores, Inc.

My background includes full responsibility for suspect surveillance and apprehension, and I have proven my ability to work effectively with staff and management at all levels of experience. Most importantly, I have demonstrated my ability to reduce lost revenues from theft or shrinkage, while maintaining a safe environment for all employees and customers.

I can provide letters of recommendation from managers. Please let me know as soon as possible when we may meet for an interview to discuss how my skills may help your company lower its losses. I look forward to your response.

Thank you for your time and consideration.

Sincerely,

William E. Winkler

encl.

Cover Letters for Professional/Management Positions

The following examples are for professional and/or management positions requiring special skills, training, or a college degree. You should write your letter at a level appropriate for the employer or position. In other words, don't be afraid to use industry terminologies that demonstrates how well you understand the position you're seeking. Employers at this level need to see that you have a good command of the language and that you can write with precision and impact. This is especially true if the job itself will require writing reports, memos, or information related to customers or products. While writing your cover letter, always think about how relevant your material is to the position you are seeking. What are the most important aspects of your background that will pry open the door to an interview and get you noticed for a specific job? This is the kind of information employers want to see in the first one or two paragraphs of your cover letter.

Sample Letter
Professional/Management
Manufacturing/Design Engineering

DONALD A. CRANE
55 Justin Court
Addison, VT 40101
208/555-7215

Ms. Naomi Justin
PBT Enterprises
20157 Randall Parkway
Middlebury, VT 05753

Dear Ms. Justin,

With more than twelve years in Manufacturing and Design Engineering, I would like to discuss how my experience can benefit your company. I most recently read about your company's acquisition of Dumler, Inc., a former client of my employer, GS Gibson.

I currently manage a design and manufacturing engineering team in state-of-the-art product and process development for a wide range of applications. I would be most valuable to you in a position requiring greater innovation and creativity, and which offers the potential for career advancement.

My efforts have resulted in major cost reductions and quality improvements for key customers, as well as for in-house operations. I can now assist your technical staff in virtually all stages of process and product development.

I can provide much more information including a portfolio of photographs of my most important work. To that end, I look forward to hearing from you soon.

Sincerely,

Donald A. Crane

enclosure

Sample Letter
Professional/Management
Business Administration

MARK J. DAVIDSON
885 Saturday Drive
Doylestown, PA 18901
215/555-9783

Mr. Richard Carter
American Charter Co.
550 N. Broad St.
Philadelphia, PA 19108

Dear Mr. Carter

With more than six years of success in business administration and operations, I feel certain I can increase your company's profitability.

My background includes full responsibility for cost-effective purchasing, vendor relations, and inventory control on state-of-the-art computer systems. I'm also skilled in general accounting, bookkeeping and payroll operations, and if necessary, I can train and motivate a team of workers in a professional manner.

Because this letter and resume give only an outline of my background, I welcome the chance to meet with you personally to discuss your particular business needs. To that end, I will be contacting you soon to arrange an interview.

Thank you for your time and consideration.

Sincerely,

Mark J. Davidson

encl.

Sample Letter
Professional/Management
Project Manager

JOHN MIDDLETON
710 West Palm Drive
Roselle, IL 60172
708/555-1804

Mr. Jim Richardson
JWP Kenyon Electric Company
100 Appletree Road
Oak Brook, IL 60521-1916

Dear Mr. Richardson:

As you will see by the following resume, I have both field and office experience on a wide variety of projects, including crew supervision at the MGM Bloomingdale's building at 900 North Michigan Avenue. I would now like to meet with you to discuss opportunities as Project Manager.

My background includes assisting in full job estimating and project management, and I would like to further my formal education in these subjects. The foremen and journeymen I've worked with will tell you that I'm very self motivated, ambitious, and quick to learn new procedures.

Because my resume is only a summary of my background, I would welcome the opportunity to meet with you personally to discuss mutual interests. Thanks for your consideration, and I look forward to hearing from you soon.

Sincerely,

John Middleton

enclosure

Sample Letter
**Professional/Management
Construction Manager**

ROBERT L. AUGUSTA
806 Floral Lane
Bend, OR 98763
208/555-0627

Dear Hiring Manager:

I am currently employed by a major, nationwide remodeling company. This company was recently voted Remodeler of the Year for the entire country by a very respected industry publication. I held the position of Installation Manager in the Oregon branch and have contributed in making possible an honor such as this.

My background includes responsibility for up to 25 projects simultaneously, using knowledge and experience gained in my company's 37 years in the business. I now seek to further my career with a company that can provide even greater responsibility and growth potential. In turn, I can offer my new employer the dedication, enthusiasm and commitment required in such a position.

I am an extremely independent worker who's at his best under pressure. I am very well liked by my fellow workers, subcontractors and suppliers. I like to think that I am personally responsible for helping create a very high-energy, positive work environment. This creates a very productive and, in turn, profitable business. I love to deal with people and take pride in accomplishing big projects and solving problems. I feel great when I can save my employer money and am always looking to take on more, learn more, and be more valuable to my company.

I would appreciate a personal interview with your firm. Given the chance for an interview, I'm sure you will agree that I could be an extremely valuable asset to your organization.

I look forward to hearing from you.

Sincerely,

Robert L. Augusta

encl.

Sample Letter
Professional/Management
Plant Manager

CASEY M. JONES
61 Ramsgate Circle North
Hanover Park, ND 30103
317/555-4294

Dear Hiring Manager:

In this uncertain economy, even in the best managed companies, there is a growing consensus that experienced manufacturing talent will prove key to profitable operations throughout the 1990s.

Through 20 years of proven success, I've demonstrated a consistent ability to contribute to profitability in all areas of production, process engineering, and leadership.

By way of example, as Plant Manager for a specialty metal products company, I've been instrumental in managing growth from $8 million to more than $30 million in a relatively short period of time. However, for reasons which I would be glad to share privately, I am looking to explore some new challenges.

Because I feel that your situation is one where my experience would fit nicely, I decided to forward my resume. If in reviewing it, you feel it merits at least an exploratory discussion, I would be happy to arrange a visit at your convenience.

My thanks in advance for your consideration. I look forward to your response.

Sincerely,

Casey M. Jones

enclosure

SAMUEL LYONS
5484 East Montana Street
Glendale, CA 50139
212/555-2791

Mr. Nelson DeVille
Head Nurse
Roanoke Hospital
1502 Central Ave.
Portland, OR 97222

Dear Mr. DeVille:

I am seeking to relocate to Oregon and fully utilize my experience as Staff RN. I have already applied for my Oregon Nursing License and am available immediately to discuss career opportunities with you.

My background includes experience in cardiac monitoring and med-surg tele units, where I developed my skills in triage, phlebotomy, and overall patient care. I am very self-motivated and am interested in pursuing graduate studies in Nursing during night courses (unless you have night shifts available.)

Throughout my career, I've proven my ability to work effectively with physicians and staff at all levels of experience. Most importantly, I have demonstrated my ability to promptly meet patient needs with a highly professional yet personalized approach.

I can provide excellent references upon request. Please let me know as soon as possible when we may meet for an interview and discuss mutual interests. I look forward to your response.

Thank you for your time and consideration.

Sincerely,

Samuel Lyons

enclosure

YVONNE BACKARA
3350 Newcastle Drive
Washington, DC 10087
Ofc. 608/555-6090
Res. 608/555-8195

Sales Manager
Widget-Makers, Inc.
40 Sellers Drive
Alexandria, VA 22312

Dear Sales Manager:

Having reviewed your most recent quarterly report, I am sending my resume and would like to explore opportunities in sales and marketing with your excellent company. Your 20 percent sales growth in 1993 tells me that your product and client services are filling a strong need, a need I can help meet while expanding your profits and market share.

My background includes full responsibility for sales presentations and marketing program development. In my most recent position with Xerox I have:

* Personally acquired over 43 new accounts, three of which are Fortune 500 firms.

* Earned three Golden Arch awards for exceeding sales goals by over 15 percent for three months in 1993.

* Trained and supervised more than twelve new sales representatives, two of whom earned Golden Arch awards.

Please let me know as soon as possible when we may meet to discuss how my self-motivation and high-energy sales techniques can help improve your company's bottom line. I look forward to your response.

Thank you for your time and consideration.

Sincerely,

Yvonne Backara

enclosure

Sample Letter
Professional/Management
Sales or Marketing Management

DONALD E. TILAN
134 Hillcrest Drive
Miami, FL 10157
348/555-3532

Sales Manager
Fieldcrest Products
12761 Enterprise Dr.
Fort Myers, FL 33903

Dear Sales Manager:

I am exploring opportunities in Sales or Marketing Management with your company. Specifically, I am seeking to better utilize my profit-building experience, which includes:

• The highly profitable acquisition and management of major national accounts, including Wal-Mart, Builder's Square, and K-Mart.

• Sales staff hiring, training, and supervision; dealer network establishment and full P&L responsibility for product development, introduction, and marketing.

• Cost-reduction, budgeting, forecasting, materials control, purchasing, and complete business startup and management.

Because the enclosed resume is necessarily a summary statement, I would welcome the opportunity to meet with you personally to discuss how my qualifications may be tailored to meet your specific needs.

Please let me know as soon as possible when we may meet. I look forward to your response.

Sincerely,

Donald E. Tilan

enclosure

Sample Letter
Professional Manangement
Field Sales/Service Rep

KELLY JONES
163 Newport Circle
Atlanta, GA 32103
438/555-1704

Nancy Andrews
M&M Mars, Inc.
520 N. Michigan #810, Dept. PC
Atlanta, GA 30328

Dear Ms. Andrews:

I am exploring opportunities as a Sales Representative with M&M Mars. My present territory includes the Far West Suburbs, and the position you have advertised seems perfect for me. Specifically, I would like to better utilize my self-motivation and profit-building skills.

As a Buyer with Jewel Discount Grocery, I worked directly with M&M Mars to coordinate seasonal and holiday promotions, and thus I'm very familiar with your product line. My experience includes major account development, and I've proven my ability to develop strong working relationships with major retailers, including Cub Foods and Revco Drug. Previous employers have said that I'm reliable, dependable, and efficient, and I believe my track record of success bears out this belief.

Because my resume is necessarily a summary statement, I would welcome the opportunity to meet with you personally to discuss your particular business needs. To that end, I look forward to hearing from you soon.

Thank you for your time and consideration.

Sincerely,

Kelly Jones

enclosure

Sample Letter
Professional/Management
Public Relations/Communications

PAULA LENNON
2406 Langley Court
Schaumburg, IL 60172
708/555-9449

Manager
Public Relations Dept.
McQuirty & Co.
Carmel, IN 46032

Dear Hiring Manager:

As Director of the Alliance Against Intoxicated Motorists (AAIM), I've developed excellent relationships with key decision makers at major businesses, as well as in local and state government. These individuals include Secretary of State George Ryan and DuPage County State's Attorney Jim Ryan. This was achieved through extensive negotiations to pass new legislation, modify existing laws, or expand public awareness on important safety issues.

Given the obvious success of your firm, I would now like to apply my experience as an active member of your team. I am seeking a position where I may fully utilize my expertise in government relations, public affairs, and/or communications.

Throughout my career, I've proven my ability to generate publicity and handle scores of interviews with print and electronic media. I have researched and written persuasive articles for local and national publications, while testifying before committees and managing a wide range of PR functions for AAIM.

I am willing to travel for the right opportunity, and will be calling you soon to arrange a personal interview. Meanwhile, please let me know if there is any further information you require.

Thank you for your time and consideration.

Yours,

Paula Lennon

enclosure

ROBERTA B. KENT
608 Carmen Avenue
Norridge, NE 30656
339/555-7564

Dr. Werner Frederick
Postalia GmbH
Emmentaler Strasse 132
3000 Berlin 51
FEDERAL REPUBLIC OF GERMANY

Dear Dr. Frederick:

Enclosed is my resume outlining my experience and responsibilities with our company. My career with Postalia has been very rewarding, and I now seek greater responsibilities in Divisional Management.

My position as National Dealer Manager requires an extensive knowledge of our dealer network. I've utilized this expertise to develop a strong camaraderie among our sales representatives, dealers, and customers alike. Through personal rapport building, communications, and motivation, my sales teams have proven to be among the best in the company.

With a strong sense of the internal and external needs of Postalia, I am confident that my talents will be an excellent resource in the years ahead. I would therefore appreciate a meeting at your convenience to discuss mutual interests.

Thank you for your time and consideration, Dr. Frederick, and I look forward to speaking with you at your earliest convenience.

Sincerely,

Roberta B. Kent

encl.

Sample Letter
Professional Management
Insurance

EDNA PEARSON
923 Aurora Avenue
Villa, AZ 27753
345/555-9929

Dear Hiring Manager:

My career as Agency Manager with Allstate Insurance has provided excellent experience in operations management, sales development, and staff supervision. I'm now seeking to increase the profitability of your company.

Throughout my career, I have demonstrated my skills in staff training, motivation, and team building. With Allstate Insurance, this has resulted in greatly expanded market share and sales volume. I achieved this by keeping a constant, sharp eye on customer service, follow-up, and the three most important areas of business success: persistence, productivity, and profitability.

I am willing to travel or relocate for the right opportunity and can provide excellent references at your request. Please let me know as soon as possible when we may meet to discuss mutual interests. I look forward to hearing from you soon.

Sincerely,

Edna Pearson

enclosure

ALBERT T. LIKEN
24 Homewood Drive
Durango, CO 81301
303/555-5636

Ms. Donna Pearson
Vice President, Finance
Helmand & Pratt
Denver, CO 80203

Dear Ms. Pearson,

I am exploring opportunities in Accounting or Finance with your company. Specifically, I would like to better utilize my leadership skills in a challenging position that offers the potential for advancement.

My background includes full responsibility for audits and status reporting. In my current position, I've proven my ability to cut costs by 20 percent, while working with staff from all departments in a strong team atmosphere. I am certain I can help improve your accounting functions while increasing your company's bottom-line profitability.

I would welcome the chance to meet you personally and discuss the needs of your business. I can provide excellent references upon request. I look forward to speaking with you soon.

Thank you for your time and consideration.

Yours Truly,

Albert T. Liken

encl.

Sample Letter
Professional/Management
CAD/CAM Drafting and Design

FARIDA C. PATEL
18 Beth Court #9
Addison, NJ 40101
878/555-7431

Ms. Susan Folke
Architect Design Services
200 W. 25th St.
New York, NY 10010

Dear Ms. Folke,

 A recent article in *Drafting World* magazine outlines your company's state-of-the-art approach to the design of customized parts for the automotive industry. Yours is the type of company I would like to be associated with. I can bring a creative, self-motivated attitude to your design team, as well as:

- Education and experience in AUTOCAD and Microstation/Intergraph systems.

- Skills in producing prompt, accurate computer conversions of manually drafted blueprints and schematics.

- A strong track record of reliability and success at my most recent position, as well as the ability to interface with staff, managers, and end-users at all levels.

I have proven my ability to work with engineers, technical staff, and managers at virtually all levels of experience. Perhaps most importantly, I have fine-tuned my ability to learn new systems and procedures quickly and accurately, while keeping a sharp eye on customer satisfaction and quality.

Please let me know as soon as possible when we may meet for an interview and discuss mutual interests. I look forward to your response.

Thank you for your time and consideration.

Sincerely,

Farida C. Patel

encl.

Sample Letter
**Professional/Management
Law Enforcement**

JANE FATICA
121 Lost Cave Lane
Grand Forks, SD 32193
328/555-6803

Mayor John Zack
Village of Oakdale
Oakdale, CA 33224

Dear Mayor Zack:

I am exploring opportunities as Police Chief with your department. Specifically, I am seeking to utilize my extensive background in law enforcement development with the Schaumburg Police Department.

In addition to more than 10 years of on-the-job experience, I can offer extensive training and certificates and commendations for professional service. Throughout my career, I have proven my ability to work with fellow officers and the community to investigate and solve a wide range of crimes. Most importantly, I have fine-tuned my communication skills with the public to help gain its essential support for law enforcement.

Complete documentation of my training, commendations, and service will be provided at your request. Please let me know as soon as possible when we may meet for an interview and discuss the needs of your department.

Thank you for your time and consideration.

Sincerely,

Jane Fatica

enclosure

Sample Letter
Professional/Management
Education/Teaching

SAMUEL E. PERCH
63 Slowdown Drive
Big Sky, MT 90101
218/555-8649

Mr. Kenneth Markus
Asst. Superintendent for Administrative Services
Roseburg School District #54
442 North Lakeview Drive
Roseburg, IL 60194

Dear Mr. Markus,

Thank you for the opportunity to be a substitute teacher in your excellent school district. I am eager to continue my teaching endeavors in District #54's junior high, Indian Trail, as a full-time teacher in the Social Science Department.

Throughout my education and numerous teaching experiences, I have proven my strong, natural skills as a teacher of history on the secondary level. My sixth grade ancient history student teaching experience at Roosevelt School, under the supervision of Susan Addelson, further confirms my effectiveness in determining and meeting student needs. In addition, I can communicate with parents regarding the special needs of their children and how to meet those needs.

My qualifications are presented in more detail on the enclosed resume, and your central office has my completed job application on file. I can provide excellent references and credentials upon request.

Please contact me as soon as possible to discuss when we may meet for an interview. I look forward to your response.

Thank you for your time and consideration.

Yours Truly,

Samuel E. Perch

encl.

Sample Letter
Professional/Management
Account Management

JEFFREY H. CROCKETT
57 Weidner Road
Deer Grove, CA 33189
213/555-3086

Mr. Robert Anderson
Anderson Marketing, Inc.
835 Lincolnwood Drive
Berkeley, CA 94704

Dear Mr. Anderson:

Because of the excellent reputation of your firm, I am submitting my resume in application for an Account Management position. Specifically, I am seeking to better utilize my profit-building skills in account prospecting, acquisition, and management.

In my position with Arty Incentives, I have proven my ability to create highly profitable, personalized relationships with key clientele at hundreds of companies. I've executed complex sales with a strong knowledge of product lines, industry trends, and, of course, the customer's specific needs.

My success thus far is a result of comprehensive research and taking an interactive role in a client's business. This allows me to design and implement customized incentive programs while always keeping a sharp eye on bottom-line results.

I am willing to relocate for the right opportunity and can provide excellent references at your request. I will be contacting you soon to arrange a personal interview. Thank you for your time and consideration.

Sincerely,

Jeffrey H. Crockett

enclosure

Alice Shaminski
1145 Marlboro Lane
Rolling Knolls, AK 49896
528/555-8976

Teacher Approval Committee
St. Patrick's Language Academy
Rolling Knolls, AK 49817

Dear Committee Members,

I am seeking Certification as an Assigned Teacher with St. Patrick Language Academy. The following resume outlines my Teaching experience with learning disabled students in Rolling Knolls.

As mother of an LD student and two college-bound students, I have proven my ability to work effectively with parents of students at virtually all aptitude levels.

My activities have included full production supervision of the Rolling Knolls High School Year Book, and I am very interested in volunteer work with St. Patrick's proposed After School Program.

Please contact me directly to arrange an interview, or for further information. Thank you for your time and consideration.

Sincerely,

Alice Shaminski

encl.

Sample Letter
**Professional/Management
Boilerplate Letter for Ad Response**

Alfred E. Plate
574 West Lanford Drive
Chicago, IL 60692
312/555-9276

Mr. Edward Smith
Director of Product Development
Monroe Corporation
598 First Street, Suite 213
Chicago, IL 60606

Dear Mr. Smith:

The position of [position name] advertised in last Sunday's [newspaper name] seems tailor-made for my qualifications. My experience with [last or current employer] involved responsibility for [several duties listed in the ad], and my efforts resulted in a 20 percent reduction in overhead for 1989. The enclosed resume outlines my qualifications and accomplishments.

I now seek to better utilize my [supervisory/design/organizational, etc.] skills with an industry leader such as [company name, if applicable]. I am willing to travel or relocate, and my salary requirements are negotiable. [You may omit 'negotiable' and give a range, such as 'upper $40s per year' if requested in the ad.]

I will contact you soon to arrange an interview. Meanwhile, please feel free to give me a call should you require any further information on my background.

Sincerely,

Alfred E. Plate

enclosure

Special Situations

The following letters are especially important for people in unique situations. Here is your chance to explain your circumstances and put them in the best possible light. As mentioned earlier, remember to research the company at your local library (or call the firm directly) and get the name and address of the person in charge of actually hiring for the position at hand (not just the human resources representative).

Like any other cover letter, emphasize your most positive attributes relative to the job. Of course, special product or industry knowledge is preferred, but if you lack this background, try writing about your self-motivation, determination, organizational skills, and/or ability to work independently or as part of a team.

If you're a reliable worker who's also a fast learner, be sure to mention this. A cover letter is a great place to sell your valuable, personal attributes, whether or not you've done them on a job. Of course, try to present these as applicable to a business operation, and you'll be far ahead of applicants who send no letter at all, or only a very general cover letter.

Tips for People with Disabilities

Because there is no consensus on whether a disability should be mentioned in a cover letter, it should be mentioned if—and only if—it has a direct bearing on the performance of a particular job. On the other hand, keep in mind that some companies may be looking to hire disabled people, and if your disability is the type that will have absolutely no bearing on the performance of the job, you may wish to use one sentence of your letter to explain your situation. Again, this should be considered on a job-by-job basis. Overall, here are some key points to consider:

1. The ability to do the job should always be stressed, not the fact of a disability.

2. As with any cover letter, it should be addressed to an individual and, through knowledge of the company, should emphasize how you are the right person for his or her particular job. Research the company as much as you can prior to writing your letter/resume, even before calling the company to discuss job possibilities.

3. If you think the position might require special adaptive devices, check with the Job Accommodation Network at 800/526-7234 to make sure you know which ones are available for your situation and that particular type of work. This way you'll be prepared to answer special questions that may arise at the interviews.

4. The American Disabilities Act (ADA) does not guarantee you a job, just the chance to compete equally. Your resume describes your past accomplishments and activities. The cover letter must get the reader's attention by focusing on special attributes, skills, and knowledge that makes you uniquely qualified for the specific job at hand. Avoid repeating items in your resume; just highlight your special qualities that connect you with the job.

5. Each job requires a slightly different letter. Avoid trying to write one that will fit all possibilities.

6. Sit back and take a look at your letter when you finish, and have someone else read it too. Put yourself in the shoes of the interviewer. Would you hire this person? If so, why? Stress the key points in the interview. If you wouldn't hire yourself, write your letter again until your interest and competency shows clearly.

Cover Letter Strategies for Former Prison Inmates

Former prison inmates need to take a special approach to job hunting. The example on the page 63 is tailored to meet the concerns of a job-seeker whose special circumstances require an approach that goes beyond classified ads and takes a proactive, highly focused approach to the job market.

Using standard local and national business directories, the ex-offender in the example has built a targeted list of publishers who deal with legal materials and desktop publishing, where his skills honed as a prison inmate would be well utilized. The letter is targeted to a specific hiring manager, and it closes by noting that there will be a follow-up call placed to the employer.

Even if the applicant is told when he calls to follow up that there are no openings at that firm, this strategy allows the applicant an entry point for further follow-up. Instead of hanging up and feeling rejected, the letter writer can ask, "Could you suggest a colleague whom I could call at another company that might need my expertise? May I mention to him that I spoke to you?" Managers in a targeted industry generally know other managers and employment trends in the field and can become referral sources for qualified applicants using innovative job search strategies.

Sample Letter
Special Situation
Former Prison Inmate

Terry Berman
1731 For Ives Boulevard
Maple Heights, OH 44137
357/555-6788

May 12, 1994
Angelo Sorrento
Vice President of Client Services
Baldwin-Corona Publishers
1831 Longfellow Drive
Cleveland, OH 44138

Dear Mr. Sorrento:

As a Senior Paralegal with seven years of expertise in legal research, desktop publishing, and the editing of technical writing, I believe I can be of benefit to your organization. I am writing to you concerning a position as Researcher or Writer with your company.

In my previous position, my most significant accomplishments include:

* Conducting paralegal research and court preparation for 20 cases involving prisoners' rights for Appellate Court presentation.

* Writing, researching, and editing a quarterly newsletter circulated by subscription to 2,200 inmates of a maximum security prison.

* Conducting classes on desktop publishing and legal research utilizing LEXIS, WESTLAW, and computerized databases for a seven-member legal research staff.

My previous employer was the Bureau of Prisons, State of Ohio, Lucasville Prison Library. During my incarceration, I received extensive training in desktop publishing and legal research, including earning my B.A. in Paralegal Studies from the University of Dayton extension program.

I have enclosed a resume for your review outlining my background in greater detail. I look forward to meeting with you to discuss the contribution I could make in your setting, and will call you during the week of May 17 to arrange a mutually agreeable time for an interview.

Sincerely,

Terry Berman

enclosure

Sample Letter
Special Situation
Retiree
Returning to Work Force

Steven M. Lasso
161 Woodland Drive
Carol Lake, ND 40188
428/555-0167

United States Post Office
Carol Stream, IL 60188

Dear Postmaster:

I am exploring the possibility of reinstatement with the U.S. Post Office.

My employment with the USPS overlapped with other employment, during which time it was necessary to hold two positions for financial reasons. I regret this because I truly enjoyed and was proud of my work with the USPS.

In June of this year, I will accept retirement after 26 years of service with IBM, and would like to discuss the possibility of joining your post office.

When reviewing my previous work record, please consider my excellent performance and loyalty. I now live in Carol Stream and would appreciate the chance to give excellent service to my community.

Thank you for your time and consideration and I look forward to your response.

Yours,

Steven M. Lasso

enclosure

MARTIN D. JONES
30 Lexington Lane
Missoula, MT 40172
218/555-2103

Mr. Ed Bruno
The Edison Group
211 W. 22nd Street #14
St. Cloud, MN 56301

Dear Mr. Bruno:

I am exploring opportunities in Sales and/or Sales Management and would like to work with your firm. Specifically, I am seeking to better utilize my talents in sales team building, staff training, and motivation.

My creativity and profit-building skills, developed primarily with Minolta Corporation, have resulted in increased market share and reduced staff turnover. My high-energy approach to business development, tempered with personalized account servicing, produces satisfied clients and repeat business. This is the type of success I am certain I can now duplicate with any company.

I can provide excellent references upon request and am willing to travel for the right opportunity. Please let me know as soon as possible when we may meet for an interview and discuss mutual interests. I look forward to your response.

Thank you for your time and consideration.

Sincerely,

Martin D. Jones

enclosure

JAMES A. BURKE
75 Berwick Place
Melrose, AK 43272
744/555-9545

Dear Hiring Manager:

My experience includes direct responsibility for staff education, as well as supervision of a wide range of operations. My work with the U.S. Marines has made me highly self-motivated and disciplined, and I've successfully trained and motivated others in both communications and daily operations:

* I've proven my ability to work effectively with leaders and work crews at all levels of experience.

* My solid record of achievement was gained by coordinating staff (and/or) tackling a wide range of projects, not only with efficiency, but with a sharp eye on detail and quality.

I can provide excellent references upon request, including letters of commendation. Please let me know as soon as possible when we may meet for an interview and discuss mutual interests. I look forward to your response.

Thank you for your time and consideration.

Sincerely,

James A. Burke

enclosure

Sample Letter
Special Situation
Basic Letter, Spanish-Speaking Applicant

JOSE GARCIA
7362 Bell Road
San Diego, CA 79879
310/555-2828

Ms. Mary L. Henderson
798 East Haven Road
West Hartford, CT, 06041

Muy estimada Ms. Henderson:

He leído con gran interés el anuncio que Uds. publicaron en *El New York Times* el 16 de enero de 1995, en el cual solicitan un administrador de oficina. Con el fin de considerarme candidato al puesto, le adjunto mi curriculum vitae.

Por los detalles contenidos en el mismo, pueden constatar que reuno las calificaciones para desempeñar a su satisfacción el puesto que tienen vacante. Desde hace cinco años trabajo en la oficina central de California Fidelity Bank, donde entré como cajero y, a través de asceusos, desempeño en la actualidad el cargo de administrador de oficina. Por lo tanto, estoy familiarizado con todas las responsibilidades de la oficina.

Espero que me concedan una entrevista a su más pronta conveniencia.

Atentamente,

José Garciá

ENGLISH TRANSLATION:

Dear Ms. Henderson:

I have read with interest your ad in the *New York Times* (January 16, 1995) seeking an Office Administrator. I am pleased to enclose a copy of my resume, so that I might be considered as a candidate for the position.

The details of my resume demonstrate that I am qualified to fill the vacant position. For the past three years, I have been working in the main office of California Fidelity Bank, where I started as a cashier and, through promotions, I am now Office Administrator. I am, therefore, knowledgable about all office functions.

I hope you will grant me an interview at your earliest convenience.

Sincerely,

José Garciá

JUAN HERNANDEZ
2320 Greenview Terrace
Boulder, CO 09898
121/555-6678

Mr. Leon Jackson
Environmental Consortium, Ltd.
345 Westcott Place
Cincinnati, OH 44534

Muy estimado Mr. Jackson:

Me dirijo a usted con el fin de explorar posibilidades de empleo con su dinámica companía. Por consiguiente, le adjunto mi curriculum vitae.

Los detalles de mi experiencia profesional hacen constatar que tengo grandes conocimientos en el campo de productos para la limpieza biodegradables. Durante los últimos trés años he sido gerente para un fabricante de productos similares. Me interesa, sobre todo, un puesto en el cual podría desarollar productos nuevos e innovadores.

Espero que me concedan una entrevista a su más pronta conveniencia.

Atentamente,

Juan Hernández

ENGLISH TRANSLATION:

Dear Mr. Jackson:

I am writing to you in order to explore employment opportunities with your dynamic organization. Accordingly, I have enclosed a copy of my resume.

The details of my resume attest that I have experience in the field of biodegradable cleaning products. For the past three years, I have been a manager for a manufacturer of a similar line. I am especially interested in a position that would allow me to develop new and innovative products.

I hope you will grant me an interview at your earliest convenience.

Sincerely,

Juan Hernández

Sample Letter
Special Situation
Woman Returning to Work

Joan Jackson
258 Old Farm Road
Dublin, OH 43217
614/555-0961

Personnel Department
P.O. Box 4325
Toledo, OH 23235

Dear Personnel Representative:

With my wide range of skills developed in various community groups and as a homemaker, your advertisement for Assistant Store Supervisor in Sunday's Toledo Times seems written with my qualifications in mind.

In addition to the information on my enclosed resume, I have greatly expanded my skills in time and money management, workflow scheduling, and project coordination. These are just a few of the skills required to run a busy home with four children, all of whom are now in college or pursuing their own successful careers.

As my resume indicates, I have been very active as a volunteer docent at our community library, and have served as president of the School Parent/Teacher Association. I've been very active in fundraising for various programs, and my communication and motivational skills resulted in over $22,000 in cash donations to our library and the TWIGS Christmas Bazaar.

Because this letter and resume only summarize my full qualifications, I would welcome the chance to meet with you personally to discuss your particular business needs. To that end, I look forward to hearing from you soon.

Thank you for your prompt consideration.

Sincerely,

Joan Jackson

enclosure

Follow-Up Letters

It is an excellent idea to send a follow-up letter after mailing a resume or completing an interview at a company. Many applicants fail to do this, so when you send a letter, you show the company that you're very self-motivated and interested in the job.

To follow up on a resume you've sent a company, you should state that you recently sent a resume to the company and name the position. Tell the reader you are still very interested in the job, and that you would like to meet with the hiring authority for a personal interview. Here you can also re-state key talents and skills that make you uniquely qualified for the job. Wait about one week after you've sent your resume before sending this letter.

A simple interview follow-up letter begins by thanking the reader for the interview and discussing important aspects of the job and your abilities. It ends by thanking the reader again for the interview and re-stating your interest in working for such a great company. You should send this letter within one or two days of your interview.

Sample Letter
Follow-up
Resume Sent

KENNETH P. HONDA
142 Dorchester Court
Ramblewood, OK 70107
438/555-8888

Dear Hiring Manager:

I recently sent you a resume and cover letter in application for the position of Sales Representative. This letter is to confirm your receipt of my resume, as well as my very strong interest in your company.

My successful, hands-on experience and education would prove highly valuable to your operation. However, my resume and cover letter can only provide a brief explanation of my background, and I would therefore like the chance to meet with you personally to discuss your particular business needs. To that end, I look forward to hearing from you soon.

Thanks again for your time and consideration.

Sincerely,

Kenneth P. Honda

Sample Letter
Follow-up
Interview/Thank You

***

Debra Roberts
897 Salem Trail #B2
Bluebrook, PA 40062
727/555-1265

Jane Alvin
Regional Sales Manager
Compaq Corporation
398 Microchip Drive
Chicago, IL 60683

Dear Ms. Alvin,

Thank you for your time and for a very informative interview on Monday. It was a pleasure meeting you, and I was most impressed by the high professional standards demonstrated by your staff.

I am certain my sales and marketing skills would prove extremely valuable as a member of your Northwestern Regional Sales Team. Your product line is excellent, and your company has proven its ability to reach both new and expanding markets.

Once again, thank you for your consideration, and I look forward to new career challenges with your excellent firm.

Sincerely,

Debra Roberts

Sample Letter
Follow-up
Interview/Executive Level

RALPH D. STEFAN
134 Crest Drive
Medinah, MI 30157
678/555-3532

Mr. Roger J. Krause
Liquid Container Company
275 Nuclear Drive
West Chicago, IL 60124

Dear Roger:

Thank you for a very interesting and informative interview regarding the position at Liquid Container. If I monopolized the conversation, it was just due to the excitement and enthusiasm I was feeling based on knowing I am the correct fit for the position.

As we discussed, I do feel that a restructure of the sales commission/bonus plans with a keen eye to immediacy of reward, skewed substantially toward repeat and add-on business, would be beneficial.

I feel intensive field support, combined with a program to establish ongoing interaction with key account decision makers, would clearly identify the new role and authority of your sales staff. This would also serve to solidify your manager's commitment to relationship-building opportunities for all accounts.

I feel my prior experience in full-spectrum manufacturing of household and auto after-market chemicals gives me an in-depth knowledge of potential customer needs, from packaging to desired consumer benefits. To put it quite simply, I know what customers want because I was previously in their position.

Through my conversation with you, I feel that the position provides exactly the type of long-term career opportunity I am seeking. I am fully confident that I will prove to be a valuable asset to you and your division, and look forward to meeting with you again to further discuss your needs and my qualifications.

Yours Truly,

Ralph D. Stefan

Reference and Salary History Sheets

It is always a good idea to have reference and salary history sheets printed in case they're requested by an employer. Many advertisements now ask that you send one or both of these sheets with your resume. Salary history sheets are especially valuable to employers who are looking for an applicant at a certain salary level. Bring copies of each of these to your interviews, in case they're requested by the employer. Always be prepared!

Follow the examples below for both of these sheets, but remember *not* to send them unless requested by the employer. This is especially true of salary history sheets, because you may come across as over- or underpriced for the position. If you are willing to work at a lower pay scale, you should add: "Current salary requirements are open to negotiation."

If an employer requests only salary requirements, don't send a salary history at all, but instead give them a salary range in your cover letter such as: "I am currently seeking a position in the range of $20,000–$22,000 per year."

When listing references, separate them into business and personal, and try to have three to five of each. Be sure to call your references first and make sure it's okay if you use their names.

Sample Reference Sheet

JOHN H. DOAN, JR.

REFERENCES

Business:

Bruce Gin, President
Fairfield Marine, Inc.
5739 Dixie Highway
Fairfield, OH 45014
513/555-0825

Brian Krixen, Partner
Ernst & Young
150 South Wacker Drive
Chicago, IL 60606
312/555-1800

Charlie Kinnock, VP Sales/Marketing
Jayco Inc.
P.O. Box 460
Middlebury, IN 46540
219/555-5861

Jim E. Shields, President
Shields Southwest Sales, Inc.
1008 Brady Avenue N.W.
Atlanta, GA 30318
404/555-1133

Personal:

Richard Baeson, Yamaha
Business Development Manager
P.O. Box 8234
Barrington, IL 60011
708/555-4446

Bob Redson, Salesman
Central Photo Engraving
712 South Prairie Avenue
Chicago, IL 60616
708/555-9119

Dan Linder, CPA
Conklin Accounting & Tax Service
5262 South Rt. 83 #308
Willowbrook, IL 60514
708/555-8800

Baden Powell, Manager
Banker's Leasing Association
3201 Lake Cook Road
Northbrook, IL 60062
708/555-5353

STEVEN A. ROGERS

Salary History
(Annual Basis)

People Search, Inc.
Human Resources Representative $30,000

Anderson Employment, Inc.
Staff Writer   Up to $25,000: Commission-Based

National Van Lines
Corporate Recruiter $24,000

Professional Career Consultants
Writer and Branch Manager   Up to $29,000: Commission-Based

Notes:

* You could also add: "Current salary requirements are open to negotiation."

If salary _requirements_ are requested, you could also add:

* Currently seeking a position in the low $20s (or $30s, etc.) per year.

Remember that this could label you as overpriced or underpriced for the position. That's one reason they ask for a salary history in the first place.

Also remember that unless you feel it's essential, include salary history and/or requirements only when requested by the employer.

PART IV

Printing and Using Your Letter and Resume

Using Your Cover Letter and Resume

Cover letters and resumes are most commonly used to respond to advertisements, but they have many other uses as well.

Networking

This is the best, if least common, use of your resume. Make sure those you know in the industry have a copy of your resume if you're out of work. Give copies to your family and friends, or anyone at all who might know a company president, manager, supervisor, or influential professional in your field. Acquaintances from professional groups and associations also can be valuable. If you are still employed and must maintain confidentiality, offer your resume only to people you can really trust, and who won't inform your boss or others at your company about your intention to leave.

Employment Agencies

Don't underestimate the power of a private employment agency or your state's job service. They often have positions that are not advertised because of the client firm's desire for confidentiality or detachment from the screening process. Register with the more established firms and avoid the sleazy operations that make promises they can't keep. Avoid paying resume writing and clerical charges disguised as "out-of-pocket expenses." Unless you really believe the agency can help you out, let the employer pay the fees. In general, never pay for a job.

Cold Calling

Drop in off the street, in business attire of course, and fill out applications at businesses in your area. Try to research these companies first and leave a resume with your application. Call the hiring authority the next day to follow up. Even when providing a resume, never refuse to complete a job application, and avoid writing "see resume" instead of valuable information. Completing the job application is your first assignment with the company, so do it!

Different Types of Advertisements

Blind box ads are used by companies that don't want to be identified, and they pay extra for the privilege. This keeps their own employees from learning about the position and lets them maintain confidentiality. This type of ad also relieves the firm of maintaining its public image by sending the ubiquitous rejection letter. Respond to blind ads if the position seems right for you, but don't expect much. You can't call or research the company, you don't know where it's located, and you can't personalize a cover letter. Don't forget advertisements in trade journals and magazines related to your field. By the way, the company placing the blind ad could be your own!

College Placement Offices

Send a few copies of your resume to the placement office at your old school(s). Even if you haven't seen the place in years, you never know what this may lead to.

Career/Job Fairs

These are great places to drop off resumes with many companies and save time, travel, and postage. A cover letter is not expected and these fairs offer the chance to have mini-interviews right on the spot. There are free job fairs at colleges and hotels listed in many Sunday newspapers. Begin with the fairs that charge no admission fee and review the list of companies before you attend.

Tips on Mailing and Follow-up

When possible, use large 9" x 12" envelopes to mail your cover letter and resume. This costs a bit more, but your correspondence arrives flat and clean. Folding laser typeset letters can actually crack the type/toner off the page, and the reader ends up with black dust everywhere. If you're responding to a blind P.O. box ad, use a standard envelope with sufficient postage, but be sure to fold your letter and resume between lines of type to avoid cracking.

Call the company on the date you mail your cover letter and resume and try to speak directly with the manager or hiring authority. If that's impossible, at least talk to the personnel representative. Tell him or her your name and that you've sent a resume in application for a position. Try to strike up a conversation about your qualifications and how they're just right for the job, but don't oversell yourself if the person sounds too busy to talk. Of course, if the advertisement or posting says NO CALLS PLEASE, then don't call—unless you can anonymously learn the hiring authority's name and/or title from the receptionist. In that case, try calling that person directly to inquire about opportunities in your field, as if you've never seen the ad and heard about the company through industry contacts or a friend. Be prepared to handle yourself well if you try this!

Keep a detailed list or card file of resumes sent to whom and on what date. You should call the company three to four days after sending your resume and try to speak with the actual hiring authority. Tell this person you want to confirm that he or she has received your resume and that you would like to arrange an interview. Try to speak directly with the manager or supervisor, but if that's impossible, try the personnel representative. However, be sure not to make a pest of yourself! Hounding anyone on the telephone is perceived as pushy and desperate.

As a personnel representative, I came across an extreme example of this problem with an applicant whom the manager and I had already interviewed. We agreed that although the candidate had energy and some degree of experience, it just wasn't the kind of experience we thought was essential to the job. After learning he had not been hired, the applicant called our office at least ten times over the next two weeks to tell us more about his background and why he thought we had a great company. He drove the receptionist crazy and only confirmed our suspicions of immaturity.

If the manager or representative refuses to speak with you or set an interview, give it one more try over the next day or two. Then sit tight or send a follow-up letter like the one on page 71. Don't be discouraged by being told "we're reviewing the applications and will be arranging interviews as soon as we've screened them all." This is the standard "don't call us, we'll call you" line, and it's not without justification. Sometimes employers really *do* want to sift through resumes first and then decide whom to meet.

The whole idea of resume follow-up is to drop your name into the mind of the manager or representative and distance yourself from the silent stack of resumes. If you can set an interview, fine. But remember that employers have time constraints and perhaps hundreds of resumes to screen, so don't be dismayed.

Motivation Is Essential

When all is said and done, you must stay motivated no matter how long it takes to get interviews. It's the person who stays persistent and positive that finally gets in the door.

Some people approach their job search with a "me against them" attitude, "them" being the prospective employer. They see only a wall of indifference from hiring managers and personnel representatives. This can be fatal to a job search. As hard as it may seem, you need to project yourself as an ally to all staff and managers at the target company. Try to act as if you are already part of their operation. Try to create a "we" scenario without being presumptuous. Remember, these are people you hope soon to be working with.

PART V

The Interview

If you manage to get one interview for every 20 resumes sent in response to advertisements, you're doing pretty well. Even if you have several interviews booked, don't stop researching, checking advertisements, and sending resumes. Always hedge yourself in case an interview is canceled. However, don't book too many interviews on the same day. Some may run two to three hours, and you may be late getting to the next one. Never be late for an interview! Leave early and allow for bad weather or traffic jams. The single most important thing to remember about the interview is *don't be nervous.*

Any decent interviewer understands that you may be nervous, especially if it's one of your very first interviews. He or she should know how to put you at ease right from the start with some light conversation, rather than put you on the spot, but don't count on it. Some interviewers actually enjoy intimidating candidates with difficult questions or tricky situations to see how they react under pressure. Just keep in mind that it's all a show to see what you're made of. Keep your composure as much as possible, thoughtfully consider your replies, and maintain eye contact with the interviewer when responding.

An interview is not a life or death situation. Relax and just be yourself. Easier said than done? Remember that you're not the only person who will be interviewed for the job. The company may be interviewing other candidates who come across as more relaxed and confident but don't have the skills and experience you have. Don't let them get the job!

No matter how intimidating an interviewer may seem, remember that he or she probably sat right where you are and answered the same questions to get his or her job. After interviewing hundreds of job applicants, I found the more relaxed the candidate became, the more relaxed I also became. I still asked the tough questions I always did, but our conversation was much more informative and natural.

Get excited about the interview as a discovery process. Be aware of whether you talk too much or too little, but feel free to ask questions about the company without appearing skeptical. Try to give the interviewer an honest impression of confidence (without being cocky), personality (without being a clown), and intelligence (without talking down to the interviewer).

If you are consistently calm and measured in your answers and the interviewer seems inattentive, overbearing, or gives vague responses to questions about compensation, work hours, or specific job duties, don't waste your time. Forget the company and find a better place to spend 40–50 hours of your life every week. Throughout your job search, no matter how hard it seems, you must always keep a positive attitude. Act professionally and courteously—with the receptionist, with everyone. Dress professionally—look the part.

The single most important thing, as with anything in life, is to keep a positive attitude. Maintain eye contact and speak clearly—on the phone, at the interview, with the receptionist, with everyone. Remember, these people may soon be your co-workers. Everyone wants to be around a winner: act like a winner.

APPENDIX A

Books and
Resource Materials

Many of the books included below cross-reference companies by industry and provide insight on company size and products, as well as the names of human resource personnel and key managers. Visit your local library and ask about these books. Also, ask your librarian to direct you to reference materials on the specific industry or business you're interested in. Many of these are also listed in an excellent book for higher-level jobseekers: *Rites of Passage at $100,000+* by John Lucht.

Cover Letters, Resumes, and Interviews

The Guide to Basic Resume Writing. PLA/Public Library Association. Lincolnwood, IL: VGM Career Horizons, 1991.

Cover Letters They Don't Forget. Martin, Eric R. and Langhorne, Karyn. Lincolnwood, IL: VGM Career Horizons, 1993.

TOP SECRET Resumes for the '90s. Provenzano, Steven. Schaumburg, IL: DeskTop Publishing, Inc. 214 pages, including 140+ pages of cover letters and resumes, 1994.

175 High-Impact Cover Letters. Beatty, Richard H. New York, NY: Wiley Press, 1992.

The Perfect Cover Letter. Beatty, Richard H. New York, NY: Wiley Press, 1989.

The Writer's Guide to Query Letters and Cover Letters. Burgett, Gordon. Rocklin, CA: Prima Publishing, 1992.

Dynamite Cover Letters. Krannich, Ronald L. Wood Bridge, VA: Impact Publishing, 1991.

Cover Letters That Knock 'Em Dead. Yate, Martin. Boston, MA: Bob Adams Publishers, 1992.

Knock 'Em Dead with Great Answers to Tough Interview Questions. Yate, Martin. Boston, MA: Bob Adams Publishers, 1992.

Getting Hired in the '90s. Spina, Vicki. Schaumburg, IL: Corporate Image Publishers, 1993.

General Reference and Research Books

Manufacturers News. Evanston, IL: Manufacturers News, Inc. State by state directories. Lists by product, SIC code, alphabetically, geographically, parent company. Also addresses, phone numbers, and FAX numbers. Includes executive titles, number of employees, annual sales, and year established. Cross-referenced by product. 200-1900 pages, published annually.

Directory of American Employment Agencies. Overseas Employment Services, Mt. Royal PQ, Canada. An annual directory that lists 850+ employment and recruitment agencies.

Encyclopedia of Associations: National Organizations of the U.S. Detroit, MI: Gale Research, Inc. Four volumes in three books, with detailed information on more than 22,000 nonprofit associations and organizations of all kinds. Published annually.

International Directory of Company Histories. St. James, available from Gale Research, Inc., Detroit, MI. Gives basic information and histories (1,500–3,000 words each) for about 1,250 companies in the U.S., Canada, U.K., Europe, and Japan.

Job Hunter's Sourcebook. Detroit, MI: Gale Research, Inc., 1992.

Job Seeker's Guide to Private and Public Companies. Detroit, MI: Gale Research, Inc. Information on more than 25,000 companies, including corporate overviews, specific job titles and estimated number of openings for each, hiring practices, personnel contacts, employee benefits, application procedures, and recruitment activities, 1993.

National Directory of Addresses and Telephone Numbers. Detroit, MI: General Information, Inc. Great for your mailing list. Provides addresses and phone numbers for U.S. corporations; updated annually.

Standard & Poor's Register of Corporations, Directors, and Executives. Three volumes with just about everything on major U.S. and Canadian companies and those who run them. Published annually.

Thomas' Register of American Manufacturers. New York, NY: Thomas Publishing Company. Annual profile of 150,000 manufacturers with their major products and services. Includes 12,000 pages of catalog material and 112,000 registered trademarks and brand names.

Ward's Business Directory of U.S. Private and Public Companies. Detroit, MI: Gale Research, Inc. Annual, four volumes. Provides demographic and financial business data on over 85,000 companies. Volumes provide listings of companies by alphabet and ZIP code.

APPENDIX B

Action Words

Use these action words to add power and impact to your writing:

Achieved	Demonstrated	Introduced	Reorganized
Adapted	Designed	Investigated	Researched
Administered	Developed	Launched	Resolved
Advanced	Devised	Lectured	Restructured
Advised	Directed	Maintained	Reversed
Allocated	Drafted	Managed	Reviewed
Amended	Edited	Marketed	Revised
Analyzed	Eliminated	Modified	Saved
Appointed	Established	Monitored	Scheduled
Approved	Evaluated	Motivated	Screened
Assigned	Expanded	Organized	Solved
Assisted	Expedited	Participated	Spearheaded
Authored	Focused	Performed	Streamlined
Budgeted	Forecasted	Pinpointed	Strengthened
Built	Formulated	Planned	Structured
Calculated	Founded	Prepared	Supervised
Collected	Generated	Processed	Supported
Compiled	Guided	Produced	Tabulated
Computed	Headed up	Promoted	Taught
Conducted	Identified	Proposed	Trained
Contained	Implemented	Provided	Trimmed
Controlled	Improved	Published	Unified
Coordinated	Increased	Purchased	Updated
Created	Initiated	Recommended	Validated
Cut	Innovated	Recruited	Wrote
Decreased	Instituted	Reduced	
Delegated	Interpreted	Reinforced	

About the Author

Steven Provenzano is the president of a successful professional resume service. As such, he has written more than 3,000 resumes and cover letters. He also consults with clients on resume and cover letter preparation, as well as working as a writer and designer.